# Book of Fire

# Book of Fire

*Cary Waterman*

NODIN PRESS

ISBN 978-1-935666-30-1
Cover painting: Charles Waterman
Design and layout: John Toren

Library of Congress Cataloging-in-Publication Data

Waterman, Cary, 1942–
Book of fire / Cary Waterman.
p. cm.
Poems.
ISBN 978-1-935666-30-1
I. Title.
PS3573.A814B66 2011
811'.54--dc22
                2011018455


Nodin Press, LLC
530 North Third Street
Suite 120
Minneapolis, MN
55401

*for*


Isabel
Aaron
Winona
Marshall
Graham

# ACKNOWLEDGEMENTS

Grateful acknowledgement is made to the editors and
publishers of the following magazines and anthologies
in which some of these poems first appeared: *Blue Earth
Review, Common Ground Review, Cutthroat, Dust and Fire,
Great River Review, Minnetonka Review, Murphy Square, New
Guard Review, New Jersey Poetry Journal, Poets Against the War,
Sidewalks, Turtle Quarterly, Water~Stone* and *What Light.*

I owe thanks to many who have given me encouragement
over the past years.

Phebe Hanson has been a long-time friend, road trip
companion, and writing pal. This book would not exist
without her.

Roseann Lloyd, sister-muse, has seen this book through its
long gestation.

Gratitude to my writing group members Pat Barone, Kate
Dayton, Martha Meek, Mary Kay Rummel, Nancy Raeburn
and Carol Masters, and to Sharon Chmielarz who helped
with the final manuscript.

Thanks to Jennette Jones who listened to my dreams and
my poems. And to Kate Green, writing partner for many
years and many journeys.

Thank you to my children Amy, Bridgit, and Devin and to
my brother, Chris, and my sister-in-law, Cindy, and to John
La Fond for always being there.

And thanks to my lively colleagues in the English
Department at Augsburg College and to my students from
whom I've learned much about beauty.

# Contents

# Book of Fire

# I

*I did know that I must keep faith
with something; I called it writing.
Write. Write or die.*

– H.D.

## PERSEPHONE'S RETURN

Where has she been, that girl?
                    Back from her winter travels
with him
        Prince of Darkness
                    outlaw

How could she not love him
        runic smile
                    muscled leather vest

and when she arched her leg
        like a question mark
                over the saddle-seat behind him,
                    encircled his sweat with her swan arms,

they exploded     spacecraft,
                booster rocket
                    falling away as they tore into deep space.

But today,
        lilacs.

She's back with us.
Mother's Day.   Demeter
                    out in the garden looking in spite of her
            flowery dress,
        bent and old.

What is it that propels the girl toward dark?

And the man who held her

He wants     He wants.

A single bird swoops low over the river
        where the Crime Scene van
                is parked beside a cop car.

They are down in the reeds and muck
        of the riverbank
                looking for clues.

A body.

Demeter can tell them.

                There has been a crime here.

## Persephone in Hades

It's a girl's job to go
        to Hades.

How he'd wake her in the dark
      his winter need      flesh
           on flesh for warmth

The dog came every morning
stood by their bed
      a trinity of heads
          birth, death and in-between
    ears   petals   paws
             gone   now   coming

The girl reached
      the dog bowed      said the girl was holy
         a visitor from another kingdom

said it was she who must lift up
      every spring
         and lay the winter dark down

Without her only
        oblivion

Said she must give thanks for all of it:

      honey-cakes for the god
         a bone for the  bitch-dog
            her dry dugs    slippery tongue.

It begins as length of light     sun ascending already

Days      like the uncoiling rose
                    stretched
                              away from winter sleep     story

And she
            *that for so long*
                    *was nothing*

first breath of bubbled air
            the world enticing love
                    tree budding bareness

branch to shoulder
                    elbow,
such whiteness each morning

anticipated
                    the opening
a ladder of stars

now, now, now, now
now

# Persephone on Mount Oberg

Hawkweed & buttercup
            under her chin

at each step a shawl of evergreen
                        settles

toes of cedar
        mother sinking into rock

the salmon red mushrooms ask
come closer    bend down
        touch    and    eat

nubbins of raspberries
trillium    wild rose    flag of yarrow

every leaf glistens
        a whiskey jay calls and calls
and the trail is mudded with paw prints
        fox    wolf    black bear

How did she get here
        the overlook where she sees into distance
                travels her breath
                        remembers winter when
her mother wept like death?

The sign says: *stay back from the edge*
        or you will be            falling
                falling

water spills down the mountain
        wind plays a cello in branches

The sign says: *keep children in hand*
heads of white lace nod
chickadee  dee    dee    dee    dee

She walked through fire to get here
rock face lichen
blue iris lake
left desire, seduction behind

birds speak of rain

reaching up from below
bones of white birch dancing

## SALVATION

How fiercely trees grow in the north,
young, long-needled firs snug against the mother tree.
Indian paintbrush, purple loosestrife, orange hawkweed
nod in early morning shade.
On the highway two motorcycles rip by her.
The edge of things favors wildness,
any disturbance a force for seed and sex.
The wild rose she saw yesterday:
gone. Just stalk and rose hips,
petals kissing grass.

Last night's rain pooled on rock schist.
Orange lichen grows a sweet face on granite.
Mist burns her history from the dark water.
The sun is here,
faithful old mesmerizing sun flaming out
one day at a time.
On the lake little floating gunboats of gulls ride the chop,
swoop for love deep inside a fish.

# In the Garden

### 1

Zeus, the dog next door,
offers up a laconic bark.
Between lattices of a bamboo cage
tomatoes climb to sun.
All things must be staked up,
the fallen lilies collapsed
like ladies in pink ball gowns,
the clematis with its purple face,
the reluctant roses.
Everything needs help standing.
Going skyward on a ladder to paint
she leans in, feel the rungs kiss her feet.

### 2

Home late, she waters plants,
falls asleep in the garden.
A dog's chain clinks her awake.
Her flowers, even though she has treated them
so well, fed and fussed over them,
begin to fail. It is almost
August, the pause between bounty
and death. Baby birds have fledged.
Grass yellows. The season turns
like the smile of a fish hook.

3

One cloud floats west to east.
In the Japanese Garden at Lake Como
Buddhists celebrate Oban,
light candles to lead home the family ghosts.

She does not wish to return there,
feels instead the high thin promise of
a whole life inside her body
even after marriage, children, divorce, death,
the space where a mother and father used to be.

She is still that same girl,
her hair on fire.


4

Last light on lilies.
It greens only the surface of rapier leaves,
the underside still in shadow.
By the garage a groundhog shuffles
toward hibernation. In the coldest months
he will breathe only once every minute.

What is there finally but gratitude?
She sits in the garden,
does nothing but watch leaves tremble,
sees slotted sun come through the fence,
opens her heart to the forgiveness of a life.
The mourning dove knows her,
comes to the feeder in steelcoat grey,
a peaceful bird with all manner of secrets
and hidden darkness.

## INFIAMMATI FIRE CIRCUS

Pulled down
        into heat of the underworld
The sun saw her go.
And thunder from the mountain

The air stinks of phosphorus
        as the night bus
hurtles down through crevices
                and magical moraines

Megadeath
oh   how she
        shakes
 the linden
      shimmy       shimmy
it's 90 hot degrees
        and rising

ghetto blaster    thump  thump    thump
disaster bumping
        down
            the street

Begin the reign of flame
      Seats available next to Demeter
      Pyrotechnics

      Dancing girls
      Shadow puppets
   Aerialists on fire:

She did not die
Remember this

She did not die

## Persephone at the Spa

She strips down to a sheet,
everything      white except fleshy
        putti cherubs on the painted ceiling.

A smocked woman says:
                *you are dry, dry*
old skin needing to be sloughed,
        needing exfoliation, hot oil,
                abrasion,
then the anointing of creams.

Like volcanic magma rises,
        the layer of summer bronze lifts,
                scraped off to reveal
                        another layer and then another.

Sediment, fossilized sandstone
        your face a monument to the wear
                of love and sex and grief.

And then the burning after
        the burning of summer,
                your mother's hot breath.

You prepare for him again,
        moist cotton patches
                sucking light
                        over startled eyes.

The esthiologist says:
                *hydrate, hydrate,*
applies Ylang ylang,
                love aphrodisiac
for the wedding,
        the winter dark.

# DESCENT

## 1

Venus coming early.
And the stars,
the young ones
and those old stars
with their old light,
what are they burning
between the thighs of solstice?

Only the dying know,
those giving over to the other hand.
What they'll miss most is the absolute blue
of sky. And crickets
singing by the fence line.
The cottonwood shakes, gives up a
yellow leaf, a woman
at the edge of grief.

Black starling watches over all,
calls the turning into place.

## 2

Muggy night.
Storms encroaching from the west.
Mosquitoes buzz in the dense field of air.

Earlier today she could not spell escape,
kept wanting to put an X in it,
obliterate something.

Tonight, she lies on her hot bed
reading poems all night.

Fan blades rotate,
swords over her old
sweat and throb.

3

Early morning in the garden,
sun about to stride around the corner.
Fat bees sip nectar from the Russian Sage.
A bee's life is one big sweetness
from birth until the moment he is pushed
out of the hive, useful
no longer.

Crow calls in this early light.
She tells what we are rushing toward.
The king of darkness stole
the girl of summer as she picked
wildflowers in the meadow,
the earth opening, taking her down.

A spider has sent one filament of
her juice down from the fir tree
to the glass patio table.
She asks:

> *what's wrong*
> *with the song of melancholy?*

4

At the end of summer
the fuzzy bumblebee goes
to each small white flower
on the stalks of sweet basil.

He is persistent, rough,
pushing his tongue into the soft folds of one
while the others bend shyly in the breeze,
girls waiting to be asked to dance.

This bee will have his way with each one
and done, will saunter off across the garden,
the taste of honey pesto heavy in his mouth.

5

She paddles upstream.
The first leaves blown from trees
and carried by the river
are all going the other way.

Suddenly, she knows
how her ego separates her
from the ladybug on the skin of the kayak
and from her own death.

Listen to the wind rise
telling of winter.
See the leaves passing
face down in the water.
No struggle,
no fear of sinking.

6

Late October light comes filtered through
the white blinds of the bedroom,
a peace in this at last,
no cloying August brightness
or damp thighs on bed sheets.

Again, Persephone descending
faithfully each fall to Hades,
lover of dark and what's underneath,
as if she could possibly want him.

But the light, this last light.
Tonight it will freeze. Basil and shrub roses
will stiffen from a sudden incursion.
As it darkens they will slump,
only a memory of what had been.

But still the light, it is lovely in its going,
playing blues on the window blinds,
tossing up leaves to Mr. Bones.

## At the Minnesota State Fair

All the girls want to be Persephone.

End of summer.
      barns full of sows     cows,
all brought by  grain and grass and sun
      to fullness.

They are destined for the highest bidder,
      old bandy-legged farmer     cloven boots.
He'll staple his earrings to    their fluted ears,
      lead them onto a silver ferry
          drive home    breed or butcher.

Outside the demonstration barns young men
      take off their cowboy shirts.
It's getting    hot    pretty bare bones
      boots    ten-gallon hats
            hip-hung jeans on
butterfly pelvis
      catch at girls passing by.

The animals wait    meditate
      breath    stillness

The sow in her pen
        sees the white wind    coming
listens for the little man
      to sing out    her name.

## Leaving the Mother

She never thought she could
but having been      so many times
        in Hades      elevator to the contagion ward
hallway to down that passes
                through bedlam,
she can be free of her
        and not look back once.


Who had her tethered?


Not him, Prince of Darkness
        lips of wildflower honey
                red orgasm of Bee Balm
                        fire on her swan neck.


Blue *bleu* Persephone sky
        Blue goddess  Virgen de Guadalupe
                Mary Mater    Black Madonna


Persephone and Demeter      daughter/
        mother the only continuance
handwork of wind and weather.


The garden adorns itself
        butterflies      cardinals      sweet-faced dahlias.
Who among us would say      no to fall
        to dark fire      to cold-blown love
                and white under ice


We head into down
        single file path through forest
crack in rock

fissure in lava volcano
            in salt     in schist      through granite seam
down between the basalt columns.

## WINTER QUARANTINE

It has always snowed,
white falling like words all day and night
speaking of stones. And stars.
Of beginning in fire-hot galaxies.
In the quarantine of snow
we sleep and dream of radishes,
thousands of radishes in dark furrows,
their green ruffled caps.

For forty days and nights angels come
snowbound, coldbound,
whisper into ears of sleepers.
The Alpine glaciers will be gone
in forty years. If a thing disappears,
does its name disappear?
If the world came into being by naming
what does extinction mean?
The glacial mass of language
slides down mountains picking up debris,
words scoop out ravines and valleys,
a moraine of words,
the names of things ground down.

Glacial stars in the early white.
Some mornings before dawn,
the still-dark is a presence, a protection.
Stars bound off the roof.
The moon is invisible,
and all things begin in fire,
something that returns and returns.

# II

*To whom do we tell what happened on the
Earth, for whom do we place everywhere huge
Mirrors in the hope that they will be filled up
And will stay so?*

– Czeslaw Milosz

## Writing in Bed

I sleep in my mother's coffin.
I just can't leave her alone.
I don't want to see what
she looks like now.
Or even then,
that March day at the Bridgeport funeral home
as my children and I stood in the silence
and I put my hand out to open the coffin lid
for one last look against her explicit directions:
*No visitation. No open coffin.*
*I don't want anyone looking at me*
*when I'm dead.*


I could not
would not do it,
not after leaving her dead in the ICU,
after the nurse turned the beeping off
and said to wait while she cleaned her up,
take out the useless tubes
so we could say goodbye.
But my brother and I said *no, no*
and the two of us held hands and ran away
through the white halls out the door
into the spring sun
We had sat with her for days,
watching as she traveled farther and farther
into her coma until she was no longer
there. And at the very end, my brother
held her head and said some believe
you can feel a soul leave through the top
of the head but I hung fast to her feet
as if to hold her back.

No, I could not disobey her after that.
So she went unseen into the ground,
down to the narrow space between cement walls
in her Pendleton suit worn for the first time
about which she said:
*If I gain just one pound,*
*it will never fit.*

## BONFIRE

She's cleaned out her files,
shed skins, papers, check registers,
tax returns for the 90's,
directions for the electric waffle maker,
receipts for drugs she needed,
auto insurance stubs,
assets, debits.
She makes a bonfire of it all.

Clumps of nests in bare trees.
Birds wheel overhead,
nimbleness of a Black Hawk.
Down here ghosts toss
back and forth in the wind.

The gnats are out and they're biting.
The sky's a dreamy gauze.
Trees twirl in fall dresses and an old blue heron
flies over from lake to river.

She doesn't own much.
Only her long legs stretched out,
bone pencils writing the weather.

## LIFE UNDERWATER

She swims the Y pool with her mother
dead years now. They look down
through new no-fog goggles,
a black stripe demarcating the lane.

The man on the left torpedoes by
with big black flippers.
He knows human feet are not sufficient
in this world.
On the other side, a pregnant
half moon-bellied woman laps
at good speed.
She is swimming for two,
the baby suspended in water
inside a body suspended in water.

In this world everything is clear, simple.
The body does not struggle
to stay upright.
There is no wind
and everything stays the same.
Or nearly so.

# Virginity

The man in the dark wool Speedo
touched between her legs as he lifted
her onto the dock at Candlewood Lake.
Her father swimming with her never guessed.
And she stayed silent.

★

Riding bareback she was the wishbone
on the fulcrum of her horse,
his spine a flyway over belly and heart,
a span of breaths and then
years and years of longing.

## If It Hadn't Been Summer

if it had only been December
        or January
if it had been ice
        snow and cold
fur coats, boots,
        mittens
                layers and layers of warmth

if she hadn't felt the way
        her heart opened
its icy harness stretching
                loosening

but it was summer in Denver
        chilled Coors 3.2 beer
                madras plaid dresses
there was no one to save her

it was bare skin
        tanned limbs
                drinks with ice singing
                        it was hot

the all-night market served up
        chips and a six-pack
                under fluorescent lights
                        sticky with bug juice

they camped one weekend
        up into the foothills
                past St. Mary's Glacier
                        a slippery bowl of summer ice

the last day he sat on the hood of the car
       broke open their last bottle
           told her all about
                the women he'd known

the next time it would be winter
       she'd be pregnant
           not able to keep up as he plunged ahead
                    through all that deep snow.

# HONEYSUCKLE

*It is a funny thing when you imagine yourself returning
into the past with the contraband of the present.*
> — Nabokov

Daughter says  *it's honeysuckle.*

Mother says *no - columbine*
        red orange earlobes
              petals on green lace

Daughter says  *her father* dead
        many years ago *told her*
              *it was honeysuckle*

although now, thinking, she says  *maybe*
        *he had showed her honeysuckle next*
              *to columbine* and

Mother, because we forgive the dead
        almost everything, in fact rewrite
              our entire history with them

so that it softens like an old scab in salt water
        the fact of their death and softens
              too the fact of us still alive

to see this sunlit June day
        mirror sea all around
              Mother says *perhaps it is*

*honeysuckle*
        even though she knows
              quite definitely otherwise

because one reckless memory ago
        he waded Rush Creek to pick columbine
          the Colorado state flower

for her after they had made love
        he on top with his feet in the creek
            she on the mud of mossy bank

before everything else happened.

# Storm Warnings

In the garden I clean pine sap from a glass table. I talk to the yellow-beaked robins, say *good morning* to one who finds a seed in the grass and flies away with it. I pull out some bright baby clover that has sprouted secretly in the night.

The Kentucky Wonder beans have poked their heads out of the soil at each leg of a metal tripod. They bend small faces together, discuss their strategy, no ropes or pitons. It will be a free climb to the black knob at the top.

The Scarlet Lake Dianthus I planted last summer is coming back again like Lazarus, while the newly planted ones are still oblivious to the possibility of resurrection. But isn't this what we all want, to be bi-annual and rise pink-cheeked next spring, our green limbs folded around us?

At the end of the day what have I done? Seen a rainbow. Watched for tornadoes north of here. Heard jets rush in before the line of storm. A cardinal in church feathers sits under the big linden. I want to go with him out of the world of memory and desire. My glass on the table begins to shake. Now the table is rocking and the red alarm of weather radio blinks like a blind man.

## Lake Nokomis

The lovers,
he, 300 pounds,
she, maybe 250,
discover they are weightless
in the water.

Beaming,
they take turns
carrying each other
within the small confines
laid out for swimming.
He lifts and cradles her
as if she were a delicate parcel of pastry
wrapped and tied with string
which he is conveying home
for a bedtime treat.
Thick rope punctuated with floats
like big white marshmallows
contains their sweetness.

From the sand, a harried mother
calls to her splashing children.
Muscled men buck and dive,
ropes of ponytails down their backs,
gold earrings and crosses and tattoos
of the blue Virgin de Guadalupe

It's Saturday.
We've worked hard for the bosses all week
to have this day of sun and splashing water.
Swallows skim the grass.
Bikini girls go by pushing
the future. It sleeps.
Or bawls.

Over our heads
jets take off, gain altitude,
sweep over the beach
as if they would scoop us all up,
as if we too were weightless,
small faces pressed
at oval windows.

# WHITE HORSE, KAUAI

White bird
sits on horse's
white rump,
picks nits, cleans
his own feathers

*Contemplate*
*the mind*

A woman bites, gives
pieces of russet apple
to the white horse, says
he's still a stallion
after all these years

*This king of emptiness*

Muzzle to fly-swatter tail,
rump to fetlock,
green grass teeth to mahogany cock.
Two egrets stroll,
white generals on emerald lawn.
Sleeping mountain receives
the rain

*When you look, it is formless*
*when you call, it echoes*

At the edge of everything
rip tides, currents,
rogue waves with no
sense of responsibility.
Return the waves to the sky.

Lay the sleeping mountain down.
Return the white horse
to his dream of you

> *Grasping emptiness results*
> *in floating*
> *then sinking*

The white horse

> *does not exist*
> *nor is it non-existent*
> *It appears and disappears*

depending on the green,
depending on the rain,
depending on the call of some far-off bird.

White stallion in tall grass
eating yellow blooms of broom-weed

> *is neither shallow or deep*

flashing flies with whip of tail,
cock-sure, one hoof,
one fetlock bending for pleasure.

# DISAMBIGUATION

In last light      a radiance      of cardinals
eleven and more      coming from the sunset

all of them princes     calling        pur dy
                       pur dy          pur dy
     servants      of the servants of God

*intentional links and*    wings low & steady
        *redirecting*    across the small backyard

to choose a new prince     apostle of gold safflower seeds

like the garlands of safflowers found in the tomb of
                     Tutankhamun

*a kind of double disambiguity which is extremely rare.*

They are a long way from Northern Canada
      where many Cree and Metis are descended

from a vatican of cardinals who appeared on their horizon
                   in 1780
reproduced prolifically
               trapping furs and converts
*a set of specific type that shared the same  (or similar)*    *name*

and provided a cardinal direction    or cardinal mark
ex cathedra    N S E and, most intuitively, W
        the dead  reckoning

*not a search where there is no  significant risk*

*of confusion*

because the dead want to say something
        about  cardinals        about ambiguity

*that you can always go back        and        modify*

your errors      which are cumulative
        and grow larger with time

like truth for example      or  words

*that do not point to a single meaning*
        *from the list of   meanings*
*but to yet another        disambiguation*

which is not the way cardinals navigate

*allowing a traveler        to choose*
and a code of honor to fix all
        resulting        misdirections

from the trees down   from the ground up
        enduring missiles      knowing the path

position of stars and earth's magnetic field
        a destination guide of their own

as in    this path        this  rock        this golden seed
        this kingdom of relations.

# III

*In the dark times, will there be singing?*
*Yes, there will be singing.*
*About the dark times.*

– Bertolt  Brecht

## January 31, 2003

Before bed, I went out into the January dark, afraid of war.
I looked for the raccoon that appeared here two nights ago,
down from her leafy nest to hunt for food.

There were prints in the new snow: human, raccoon.
Under the pine tree I left a piece of chocolate cake,
an offering of peace from a country headed for war.

Out on the Iowa prairie, my dying mother-in-law prepares
                           for her 95th birthday.
Housebound now, she watches CNN all day long from her
                           snug living room.
She's been down this road so many times before, the practice
                           of war familiar.

Outside the raccoon snuffles through the dark.

## LAKE SUPERIOR SPRING

### 1

Spires of ice
along the shoreline.
What's been frozen
over the long dark months
is slowly falling,
small chimes released.
At sunset three-quarter moon
over my left shoulder.
Over my right, the sun
hanging just a moment
before disappearing
behind trees.

### 2

No wind.
The moon a white grapefruit,
haloed.
Three planets spread in an arc
toward the west.
The world is here
asking for my hand.
No one knows what happens
when we die.
Only that the spirit is released
from the weight of flesh
like an astronaut leaving
earth's gravity.
The moon reflects
rough ice of the lake,
lanterns under water,
waiting.

3

Suddenly I can hear the ice!
At first, I think it's a boat,
but everything is frozen for miles out.
It's the ice I hear,
alive,
doors opening.
All night under moonlight
the ice melts,
rubs bones against
the dark wind,
breaststrokes toward shore.

4

Today
the ice gives in
to the sun and wind,
begins to groan and crack.
Under trees, tracks
and scat.
An insistent jay scolds.
Two days without news of the world.
I don't know if we've begun
the bombing.
Here at dusk,
purple light,
everything eating ice.

## Preparing For War

There is a parcel of light,
a white cardboard box
we wake with in the morning,
search through on buses,
cradle at busy street corners.
A light we carry tucked
between arm and body
into offices, shops.

Even the sergeant
teaching war next door,
in the next building,
next grassy camp,
even he has wakened with this light,
has wiped cobwebs from his eyes,
splashed water in the morning jungle.

He has leaned with it
across the breakfast table
to kiss his wife,
rifle-fire banging in his head.
And she in her nightgown
and loose slippers
leans back into the jungle canopy,
camouflages her light with mist,
speckled leaves.

# WAR IN SPRING

*As a woman, my country is the whole world.*

—Virginia Woolf

1


A Downy woodpecker is dead on the front steps.
Last night we heard the porch windows shudder,
thought it was wind although the wind had died down.

The dead woodpecker is beautiful,
black and white confetti feathers,
a scarlet crown like a high priest might wear,
a visiting dignitary from another country
where the language is tonal,
rising and falling on breath.

It is not good to have a winged creature dead
on your doorstep.
I had seen the pair of woodpeckers yesterday
high in the cottonwood
speaking to each other, a courtship.
Now one is dead on cement,
met glass, met dark,
the sound of sonic boom
as feathers passed through time.


2


After the Bunker Busting bombs hit
what is pulled from the crater
where the house used to be?
A child's body.
Parts of a woman.
Who is responsible for this?

Not the child.
Not the woman.
Tonight half moon in the early dusk.
Whose face is silhouetted in the sky?

Three days after I find the dead bird
I dig a hole and bury him.
He doesn't look so beautiful now.
I put him down among the tulips and daffodils,
their leaves released from underground,
green hands rising.


3


After the bombing the child will soon be dead
from burns and septicemia.
A doctor will cry as he amputates
the charred arms, one burned off to the elbow.
The boy will not feel much pain,
his nerves destroyed by fire.
He doesn't know his parents, brother,
and sisters are dead.
He is in the sixth grade.
Favorite subject: geography.
Best sport: volleyball.
What does he want to be
when he grows up?


4


In the top of the fir trees
the wind is a huge hand
rocking the earth cradle.
Birds speak syllables of air,

glide from feeder to tree,
cardinal pairs,
a trio of robins in the rough grass,
all spinning headlong into spring.

The air on my skin is cool.
There is much to be done,
raking, planting, the nurture of green.
Even though I feel like I will live forever
I know it is not true,
but only some falsehood that crept over me
while I slept safe from any bombs.

## DRIVING THE OLD KASOTA ROAD ON SPRING EQUINOX

Down the black river road,
water a necklace around tree trunks,
straw matted on pale ground.

The doe is crumpled from the night before,
folding back even now into dead grass.
Balance, when the wolves are equidistant,
when all things hug the center.

I am both held and let go,
both melancholy and filled with love.
My life pools in dark water
beside fence posts on this wet night journey.

From the west a boat of darkness
pushes against dropped sky,
black against blue.
I look for you, look to tell you.
I forgive!
I am forgiven!

# Blood

Tonight red clouds streak the western Minnesota sky.
On the other side of the planet
a bombing run over Baghdad,
flames glaze the horizon.

★

Today in the bathroom at school
one drop of menstrual blood on the white toilet seat
left by the young Muslim woman,
her head covered with a scarf
who neatened herself before the mirror.

★

When my mother-in-law died in her chair,
her TV on full blast to CNN's bombing of Baghdad,
her head slumped suddenly to her chest,
blood pooling in her right cheek,
a bruising that would not go away.

# THE MICE

*For the Greeks, who had no word for irreversible death, one did
not die, one darkened.*

— Mark Strand

Where the Japanese iris right
      now stand green and ready
            to accept the inevitable
                purple blossom

she found four dead mice
      in their nest of dirt and fur
            all with their small ears pointed like pilgrims
                toward the trunk of the old cottonwood.

What happened here?
      Cat? Owl? Dog? A silent disease?
            Or had they frozen one night as
                the air fell back to winter?

Their bodies were soft as she picked them up
      unsure of whether to leave them buried, let them
            melt back to earth, first fur, then intestine,
                vertebrae, and finally small pocket of skull.

She put a rock over them but came back later,
      removed them to a black plastic bag, afraid
            of something, some disease, that the cat
                would chew on them, get sick, maybe die.

Now where the grave was there is a space
      in the clump of iris,
         darkness,
            an open mouth.

## NAPALM, 2010

After we read the poem about the Vietnam War
and how the young girl on fire ran toward the
photographer,

    *napalm/stuck to her dress like jelly*

the boys in class explain how to make napalm.

It's so easy, one says, just mix
gasoline and orange juice.
Everyone knows how to do it.
They're nineteen, twenty,
born long after the black and white photo
curled into flame and

    *Wings/beat inside her until she rises*

One says:
I made some in my driveway
and rode over it with my skateboard.
Another says: we just lit ours in the backyard
and watched it burn.

    *The lie works only as long as it takes to speak.*

Watched it burn that afternoon after 10<sup>th</sup> grade.
Weren't you afraid? I asked.
Your skin would have peeled off like bark split by steel,
an old woman beating the flames,
the pilot blinded inside his cockpit,
and the photographer with only the flash of film
to put out the fire of your burning.

## DREAM OF THE VIETNAMESE ORPHANS

At the airport I dream of the Vietnamese orphans
killed years ago in the plane intended to save them,
Operation BabyLift falling from the burning sky
just days before Saigon fell to the army of Ho Chi Minh.

Still on the ground it is easy to embrace
the nonsense of this,
their eyelashes singed off, the skin-dark burn.
Toddlers were strapped into temporary seats,
small feet reaching only to the edge,
the city on fire reflected in the dark planets of their eyes.
In the plane's cargo hold, rows of infants lay
three to a box as the plane accelerated,
rose up from the napalmed jungle
and the dead there.
*Eurasian. Dust of life.*
The twin brother who survived
the crash, the sister who died.

We try to fix our mistakes but they stretch out behind us
like phosphorus. Those babies lifted up on fumes,
jet fuel burning behind them,
we would take them home
to mothers and sisters,
to wives even,
the pool of their mothers' blood
counting for nothing.

# Failure

*I have yet to complete my casual visit to oblivion.*

— Mahmoud Darwish

In the news today another man
asked forgiveness for another war,
for his failure and the failure of others.
There was dust on the rose petals,
ash on the foreheads of those
who survived.

In my dream I am asleep
in the old car.  My father drives his Studebaker,
my head resting on his thigh.
Awake I go through the morning papers.
Bodies will never be found.
Star matter now. Ash matter.
Something raps the bowl of my heart.

I do not want to go to oblivion,
do not want to visit there.
Stone on stone,
women with their skirts pulled over their heads,
men with no right hands.

## EXECUTION

Outside, June birds sing the coda
of their delirious goodnight song.
My granddaughter finally falls asleep
in my lap as we sit in the rocking chair.

Yesterday, a young man was beheaded in Iraq,
a translator, blindfolded, kneeling.
He understood everything the masked executioner said
before the final word of the sword.

My granddaughter's hand opens and closes.
Earlier, she had tried out her sounds,
pure notes of language rising.
How much does it cost for us to be able to do this,
for me to sit here rocking, watching her sleep?

I get up and lay her in the crib.
She sighs once before turning to sleep
like all the babies of the world
who have done the human work of this day.

# IV

*Everything appears one at a time, at great distance:*
*one yellow wildflower, one brown bird, one white horse...*

– Bill Holm

# MIDNIGHT SUN, ICELAND

*for Bill Holm*

I haven't seen the dark for two weeks.
Daylight at one a.m.
and the mind does not think of night,
the absence of darkness,
does not miss it as if
it could stay light forever,
maybe what God meant when he said,
*Let there be light,*
separated day from night,
the waters divided,
the kriya cried and Mt. Tindastoll rose up
out of the fjord.
At three a.m. it is the color of birth water,
rose aureole of breast.

Dear God, how many mornings will we have like this one!
How earth blessed we are. Water blessed.
Mountain blessed. Lupine and dandelion blessed.
Blessed with the juice of roast lamb and the kindness of sheep.
And blessed by the lover of the fjord in shirt, shorts, and bathrobe,
Snorri Sturluson resurrected, poet, warrior,
sneaking the forbidden filterless cigarettes,
dreaming of sagas, looking out on the pink,
magenta, rose, peony coming toward him.

## POLAR BEAR

He had drifted with the ice wherever it took him,
a male maybe three or four years old,
then swam a long way when the ice floe melted
somewhere between Iceland and Greenland,
his paws propelling him forward,
his hind feet steering the great body like rudders.

No one knows how he got to the valley
where he was found, how many miles he swam,
how hungry he was before he was shot.
He had tasted a farmer's lamb
and wanted more. He stood up
as the county-designated bear hunters
approached with rifles from the highway.
He smelled the new beast coming toward him,
something sweet and fat.
Fog moved in from the Arctic Sea.
If they waited, he would soon be invisible.

No one understands how he came to be there.
Maybe he was an apparition – this largest of eaters –
not really a fur white bear with black skin underneath,
paws like snowshoes and non-retractable claws,
but a messenger, a collision of particles
traveling at the speed of light when they sing and split –
the explosion at the beginning of the universe.

## HÓLAR, ICELAND

In Hólar, the Bishop shows us around.
A stone wall surrounds the medieval church
and the graveyard where adolescent boys
go at the grass with industrial power trimmers.

Ratcheting up the racket
they mow down everything in their path
like the young always do, around the graves,
Bjarnason, Jónsdóttir, Sveinsson,
cut, cut, cut lush stalks of dandelions,
nests of wild thyme.

The day flies off into pieces.
We follow the bishop into the sanctuary
where lithe-limbed Jesus hangs on his cross,
one foot placed over the other
and stitched together by an iron nail.
On the rood screen paintings of the Virtues:
Faith, Hope, and Charity with her grey-veiled face.

# ECONOMY

The eider ducks are nesting by the Arctic Sea in old rubber car tires that have been set out for them by the down collectors who identify their tires with small, colored flags. The female duck sits obediently in her tire-nest, a good housewife, and pulls the down from her breast to soften the tire and cocoon her eggs. Tomorrow the down collector will come to the nest, gently slip his hand under the small body, remove a bit of down, a pinch worth, a thimbleful. For days the duck will continue to pull her own heat to provide for her ducklings. And the down collector will continue his collecting. And this is how duck and human have conspired to coexist here for centuries, the duck keeping the human warm, the human never taking more down than the duck is willing to give. A pure economy, this giving and taking.

# THE SKULL

At the edge of the North Atlantic
beside Iceland's Ring Road
I find the sheep skull.
I pose it for photos by saxifrage and butterwort
and by the pink toes of wild thyme.

I leave it, walk to my car,
then turn around and go back.
The skull becomes a perfect traveling companion,
a partner in the passenger seat of my small rented Yaris.

She doesn't say much so it's almost like
being alone, but not quite.
I photograph her at a glacier's edge
and at the tiny church at Skaftafell.

We drive through miles of black lava.
She sees the spearmint-green icebergs dip
under the Jökulsá River bridge.

She visits the Blue Lagoon,
mixes with a crowd of Japanese tourists,
wants her own terrycloth robe.

After a long day of travel,
she rests her head on a blue geothermal pipe,
hot artery from the heart.

I bring her into my last hotel room.
She watches me over breakfast
of toast and rhubarb jam.

Finally, we say goodbye outside the airport.
I can't take her with me
no matter how much I have fallen
for her dreamy eye sockets,
her toothy, innocent grin.

# AT THE CULTURE HOUSE IN REYKJAVÍK

The documentary begins with shaggy-maned horses
crossing the barren interior. The riders stop.
The narrator tells us they have come
to a horse graveyard.
A boy in the front row moves over an empty chair
to sit closer to his mother.

Later in the film, hunters wear great ruffled collars
of dead puffins around their necks.
Caught like balls in long-handled nets,
the puffins soon appear without their good looks
on a platter at the hunters' dinner table.

And the eider ducklings love the man who feeds them
for their down. They follow him,
a long line of fur balls, into the pond
and out, surround him as he lies
motherly on the grass in his checked shirt.

Upstairs in the restored scriptorium we are told
the first step to prepare for writing
was to convert animal skin to vellum:
soaked, limed, scudded and finally stretched.
Powder for ink nests in clamshells.
Seagull wings make quill pens.

Outside the Culture House, it rains
all day on the billboard of children's faces,
on the cod in the harbor,
the swans in Tjörnin Lake,
on all giving and taking in this hard landscape,
edge of the world where light begins.

## CLIMBING HVERFJALL MOUNTAIN

All things want to live.
The tiny juniper, the wild pink thyme,
        the pair of teal that circle the lava field.

I walk from Dimmuborgir to Hverfjall through pillars of lava,
then start straight up the mountain of black sand.
        My heart beats a tattoo in my chest.

I stop for breath. Then go on. Then stop again.
I am the old woman climbing to the crater
        to look down into the mixing bowl of the caldera.

At the top where it seems nothing should grow
there are white flowers in the lava
        and soft mounds of moss-like skullcaps on rock.

All things want to live. The biting midges want to live,
and the big bumble bee flirting
        from flower to flower.

My heart continues to thump
like someone stepping around a puddle
        on the way to her execution.

It occurs to me that I might die.
And I think, yes, I will.
        But probably not today.

The hike back seems easier and shorter, although
I know it's not. I add three rocks to a cairn,
        two for going out and one to come back.
            And then it begins to rain.

## THINGS THE SEA THROWS UP

Seagull wings, trapezoid of bones and feathers.
Lavender shells of Icelandic mussels.
Kriya whose nests I did not disturb.

Eider ducks that murmur together,
oohs and aahs,
and hunch on the shore
like rocks, hand grenades,
black and white semaphores,
signaling they are just ducks
with no destiny except to fill
someone's pillow and comforter.

A fog bank that rolls all the way
down Skagafjördur from the Arctic Circle.
past volcanic thrones and altars.

A length of extinct fisherman's net.
Palladium of water and sunlight.

A rusty anchor with octopus arms.

In the middle of the night it crawls toward the village,
then slinks back to the edge of the water at dawn.

## Driving the Ring Road

A black sheep by the side of the gravel road.
No. Just lava.
Dirty Pants. Scoria.
Old volcanic bombs
loose, sharp, and hard to cross.

&starf;

A sheep is nothing like a rock.
They scamper away as the car approaches,
ewe first, then lambs following her bleat,
the lambs almost always twins on this high pass over Trollskagi
where I step out in rain and climb to glacier snow,
the melt running down crazy
for the sea.

&starf;

How much farther to drive?
Just go.
It won't get dark.
I'm on the other side of the moon,
not tethered to the real life,
only fire and lava,
*geysir* and hot pot:
Bardarbunga, Loki,
Hekla and Surtsey.

&starf;

At Mývatn Lake I wake to brightness
having dreamt of an old lover
and think it's time for breakfast.
But I've read my watch upside-down.

It is only 2 a.m.
in a lunar landscape
the pillow next to mine
still smooth and plumped.

★

South towards Höfn I stop to take a picture:
two roan mares and a foal.
One mare comes toward me but the others
trot away down the fence line.
When I get back in the car news in Icelandic replaces rock music.
I hear recognizable words: Pakistan, Afghanistan, Al Qaeda, Taliban
and think something has happened.
The announcer repeats the words over and over,
Pakistan, Afghanistan, Al Qaeda, Taliban,
a litany buffeting the robust Icelandic.
I don't understand anything else.
I'm worried. Then I notice along the road
young cedar trees planted,
hundreds of them,
and I just drive on.

★

At the Hotel Alden in Seydisfjördur
three honey-wood tables along the far wall,
each with a pink vase holding
one vulva pink tulip. They all lean the same way,
toward the window and the fullest possibility of light.

But there is art and there is artifice. We're served
Smuckers jam instead of Icelandic housewife rhubarb spread.
Yogurt instead of skyr.
Something that looks like Cheerios.
They are Cheerios.
Still, the waitress goes to each empty table to spread a lace cloth.

She checks to make sure the right side is up
which is difficult to tell with lace.

At the next table three guys talk about an art student
who got pregnant, had an abortion,
then painted her final project with her blood.
They argue about whether it's art or not.
One says yes since it was intentional.
One says no but I can't hear why.
One is silent.

At the Culture House in Reykjavík
I saw the medieval books, law codices, the Poetic Edda,
Egil's Saga, laid open in a dim room
where the red eye of temperature and humidity
twitched over everything. In the dimmest corner
was the palm-sized Margretar Saga,
copied by hand and placed on the thighs
of women in childbirth
to ease their labor or hasten it.

     *

On the way to Skalanes I abandon my car.
Only stones, sheep, waterfalls, kriya,
the fjord licking the shore,
fallen houses, barns.
People were not meant to live in towns.
That's when the trouble begins.

     *

Speaking Icelandic the woman at the Hotel Framtid
says the African violets are called 'Paulina'
and her husband also leaning over the pot of purple flowers
points to the big leaves and says in English,

*no water*, and I exclaim *yes, yes*, now we can communicate,
never water the leaves of the African violets!

Then I see the photo of the hotel in winter,
the harbor clogged with ice,
the violets at the window.

★

A boulder has bounced down Skaftafell
on its way to the center of the earth
and caved in the walking path to the glacier.
All things are impermanent
and habit steals time.
Mushroom spores pulse into day.

★

In the glacial nave of Hallsgrimskirkja
sunlight comes through windows,
the glass clear so that we see clouds passing over in blue.
The pews are mountains rising out of the sea-slate floor.
A priest wears green and gold vestments,
and a young woman with her head bowed praying next to me
has black runes tattooed on her neck.

The church is the color of whitefish, cod,
and the choir a sea of singing.
Their voices swell out over the cold waters,
each one a rising, then falling wave
rolling into the North Atlantic,
over icebergs and shipwrecks
to the edge of the world.

## BECAUSE

I could not stop for every waterfall
for every ewe with twins like furry bullets dancing on grassy fields
for every shaggy mare and foal
for every black curled ram with bassoon horns
each one a venture capitalist of paternity
for every eider duck nested in down
because I could not stop for every mountain
for every glacier
for all the kriya and all the wild pink thyme

Because I could not stop
for every ice-blue mussel shell
for every golden hair of seaweed
for every cloud
for every sheep skull
for every dirty tuft of wool caught on rock
because I could not stop
for every ! sign
Vatnajökull glacier on one side of the road
nesting swans and the north Atlantic on the other
rams scratching their horns on the yellow-striped snowplow posts

Because I could not stop
for every clump of royal lupine
every phallic stalk of rhubarb
for each river with a one-lane **do-not-meet-head-on** bridge —
    I drove slowly on mountain passes with no guard rails,
    loose gravel, a corkscrew going up,
    ghosts of snow at the top
    then switchback after switchback heading down
    as I sluiced like the waterfalls
    sliding everywhere to the sea.

# V

*What is the knocking?*
*What is the knocking at the door in the night?*
*Is it somebody wants to do us harm?*
*No, no, it is the three strange angels.*
*Admit them. Admit them.*

– D. H. Lawrence

## How It Begins

Listening to Brahms's Intermezzo in A Minor
composed after he was 60,
I unbutton my shirt,
slide my fingers through my skin
and slowly separate my ribs.

Then gently, but definitely,
I push my ego
away from my heart.

# The Memory Palace

Memory, the first loss implying all others: she's already confused
Hardy and Bridges, not remembering who wrote
       "Snow in the Suburbs,"
thumbing back through her college anthology,
              pages yellowed like old piss.

     ★


After memory goes: then love, affection,
the past thin in the thin places, a run in a nylon stocking:
the space once introduced grows and grows,
              the past nodding off, cigarette still lit.

     ★


She cabled her house and car keys to the straps of her purse
so they are never forgotten like her previous keys,
lost, slumbering in the snow between
              her back door and the garage.

     ★


Mnemosyne: lake of memory, Mother of Muses,
inventor of words: without her nothing is named,
nothing remembered: shell, storm, time,
              atom collider, nothingness.

     ★


In the 6th Century Simonides constructed his Memory Palace:
salons, porticos, kitchens, a place to live with as many rooms
as what needed remembering, each room a calling forth:
              elegy for the Spartan dead,
              dirge for Danae adrift on a mirror sea.

     ★

In Thessaly Simonides stepped outside when a great wind blew
bringing down the roof, pancaking everyone at the party
to a thick batter: skin, sinew, muscle, bone and blood,
                    cups released from ringed fingers,
                    gossip from lips.

        ★


Mnemonics: faces linked like ballroom dancers hand in hand
joined what preceded to what followed: Simonides
identified each smashed guest, according to their seat at the table,
                    saying this one I remember here,
                    this one over there.

        ★


Hades. Shall we go in? Flashing lights and siren. And what sweet
food and drink shall we have in the darkness? Pomegranate seeds,
red-stained fingers, lips marking us chosen: yes, let us go,
                    but do not drink from Lethe,
                    river of forgetfulness.

        ★


She drives to the wrong place, rolls down the drafty highway,
an arsenal of forgetfulness. She plugs the stop and waits. No one
but pigeons and full busses of unremembered faces:
retreat, retrace, fill in the path going back, the memory map,
                    neurons, circuitry, full blast
                    lightening every valley and thirsty river.

        ★


But what's the rush? An ambulance hurries over snowy streets
ferrying the chosen. Let's gather at Lethe with picnic hampers,
chicken and champagne, lift our glass to what's left over:
                    bones, corks, the unwrapping
                    of all you remember.

★

Dream: she is in France, crosses a river, realizes
she can't remember the moments between departure
and arrival, doesn't know if it's spring or fall,
if the river filled with dark boats
                                        rises or descends.

        ★

In 1500, Matteo Ricci went to China to teach the Chinese to
build a Memory Palace, store an image for each thing they wished
to remember: astronomical records, the names and wages of
generals, each move in a game of Mah Jongg,
                            wounds of the crucified Christ,
                            their own stigmata.

        ★

She's lodged in her head for half a century two of Aquinas's Proofs
for the Existence of God: senior year high school theology class,
black cassocked Father Shearer, the only man allowed
                            on the all-girls school grounds.

        ★

The First Proof, Prime Mover: Simonides excusing himself
before the roof fell, a cataclysm put in motion at the beginning
when his soul was slapped into memory at birth
                            to name those crushed by the fact of stone.

        ★

What are we if not all memory? What if she did forget
everything, her mind emptying like Pandora's Box?
What if she were blowing away, scraps of paper down the street
chased after, almost captured: the whimsy wind lifts,
blows her along. Who remains empty watching her go
                            around a corner,
                            disappear from sight?

★

Someone had to begin, had to wind the clock and set it
tick-tocking: the second proof, Ultimate Good,
the phoenix of memory, to know God against which
she measures her own frailty,
                    her own gains and losses.
        ★


All her years of agnosticism and forgetting have not erased this proof.
Like grasshoppers in a night garden they wait to be stepped on,
their old tobacco-juiced bodies even now under the palace
                    of all that unremembered snow.

## VARIATIONS ON SMALL

### 1

Dirty coffee cups cluck like chickens.
And a fat black fly is trapped
on the frozen window.
Get the swatter.
This insignificance.

Outside under wind grubs
grab and bite dirt.
Above them birds close
their bits of eyes.

These are not small things
just as the light from anonymous windows
is not small,
only precise as it carves
its place out of darkness.

### 2

Days roll out from under us,
a slap to one side,
then the other,
calliope clattering
toward night.

Some days I want to know everything,
want to stride roughneck overland.
Only my breaths remain small,
the fulcrum on which
the beast turns.

3

The days are a knotted rope
of incidents,
one bumping the other along
until we fall at the end
into a place in which we fall forever.

Still, spring swells in the doorway.
Cats lose their winter fur.
Where is the string
that holds a cat together?
That holds all cats of all time
together, an unbroken circle,
their little heads bowed, their
resonating purrs?

At night we turn toward
the white sleep of chrysanthemums,
sleep like a tongue licking
smally, the way a cat does.
First paws, then face,
saying I will never love you
more than this,
never less.

# THE BAKER'S APPRENTICE

Beyond a glass divider
the girl with red hands is stirring
a bowl of dough.

She has on the vestments of baking,
white jacket and pants, dark net over
coal-black curls.

Her bear-paw hand holds a jar of peanut butter.
She spoons it into the bowl
along with a splash of vanilla.

The old wooden spoon begins the circle dance.

Tonight more snow and again the next day.
Now the oats go pouring in,
make a fist of stickiness.

Then it's all scooped out, dollops
on the greased baking pan, tiny breasts,
low hills of sweetness.

Late afternoon dusk approaches.
The city's homeless look for a night's shelter.
And some of us admit finally we do not know much.

The doughy kisses wait for the oven,
sit obligingly with no fuss.
Soon she will pull down the drawbridge of heat,
slide the pan in,
                close the metal door behind them.

## CERNUNNOS

Eight-tined god
waiting just before dawn
at the side of the highway.

Then blood and fur exploding,
a car bomb going
80 mph along Interstate 494.

Carnelian red everywhere,
white ropy intestines,
jewelry in the early morning frost.

# THE LABYRINTH

*It is solved by walking.*

        – St. Augustine of Hippo

*for Amy*

1

What story is buried inside the snaky
mounds of the labyrinth?

Tonight, grass glistens with frost.
And the fallen leaves from the old maple tree
that have collected in this winding path
whisper into their dry, thin hands.

My wool clogs leave prints on the snowy path.
By the statue of Mary
I find a squirrel-chewed pill bottle.
It says, *Traditional Chinese Medicine: Headache Ease.*
Someone has draped Mary
with a rosary of turquoise beads.

My mind is very busy today,
ricocheting.

Then I stop, suddenly
and for no reason,
take a long breath.
The snow continues.
I can hear it.
And the four a.m. dog of my life
clicks his nails across my heart.

2

Every time it is the same.
I step onto the path and begin to think
        *I am going somewhere.*

There is a destination
as in any journey.
But I go in
only to come back out
        *the same way*
except it is always different.
I swear
        *I've never been here before.*

Today I have company,
another pilgrim on the path.
We are like two horses each pulling
        a cart of accumulations:
        *memories of children*
        *torn ticket stubs*
        *strands of our dead hair*
        *the time we fell back on the grass*
                *and loved the sun.*

When we meet
        she is going one way,
I, another.  We each step
        from the center of the path to pass,
blue air a veil between us.

There is nothing else
on this curved path
where we are constant wanderers
hurtling through time and space.

I move toward the six-petaled center.
It is Epiphany.
Crows gather in the cold oak trees.
Underfoot, leaf mash and smudge of snow
still bearing
    *the memory of all the others.*


3


Today I trudge uphill
although the ground is perfectly flat.
Just when I think I'm done
there's one more revolution,
one more initiation.

Men working nearby pack up their metal lunchboxes
and move hooded and gloved to cars.
The January dusk encroaches.

This is when we must love everything brown,
dun, umber, bracken,
bone, and frozen earth.

What was it that squirrel wanted
as he sat on his haunches,
stretched his paws toward me?
Who dressed the arborvitae
in their little burlap coats?

Even in this time of deep silence
everything gives itself to us
over and over.
The sere forsythia branches
against a stone wall.
The pair of mallards swimming

in their small pool of open water
encircled by relentless ice.

Snow in the labyrinth.
On the path the wet indent of paws
and human boots.

There is only one way in.
Only one way out.

## The Marriage

Today I marry the Great Blue Heron
with striped epaulets on his wings,
both of us inside the great breathing
of cloud and earth and sky.

He is standing over there,
my beloved husband
where I can't see him
in the reeds behind the adolescent tree.
My body swells with happiness,
everything passing through
this membrane of skin.

The sky prepares for rain.
There is nothing to fear.
Low hum of first frogs,
calliope of red-winged blackbird.
Soon they will come
looking for me,
the others to whom I belong
like the iron bolts holding
the weathered picnic table together.

## Love Calls

In the still dark of Sunday morning she's awake,
snow piled around the house like surf, a lake of cold
where nothing moves. Not the child's snow angel
under the frozen lilac.
                        Nor the ghosts of roses
pricking through blue degrees below zero.


She's thinking of the poem, "Love Calls Us to the Things
of This World" and her own poem written years ago,
how she sent the women away from the laundromat,
the whine of motors, the tyranny of quarters,
to wash at a river, spread children's socks, shirts on rocks.


Today she's up earlier than the poet who woke himself
to look out as the sheets and blouses filled with air.
She's thinking of the clothesline on Hickory Street
when she was first married, a young wife fresh and sweet,
her love already unraveling.
                        Her husband came one morning,


        to say he was sorry after a bad night, found her
among their clean laundry dancing on the clothesline.
He held her
                and forgiveness swirled their sheets around them
filled with wind as if to lift them both up, laughing, to fly,
saying nothing matters more than this moment in the garden.


This was such a long time ago and she wonders why
she remembers it now, her husband dead and she living
a different life. She does not want to think
about this, wants something else,
another history, someone else's memories.

The Sunday sky lightens. Such a long life.
So many thoughts rising on a January dawn, appearing
as lost souls calling us back, insisting on their place among
the living, held in the difficult balance of earth and time
like clean white sheets and pillowcases on a line.

# BLOOD WEDDING

*for Lew Holden*

Your wife had left you post-diagnosis
yet here you were this night stumbling on fire
with dance and blood, learning the new syntax
of multiple sclerosis.
It burned from your hands and feet,
the castanets, the dark mole
on the flamenco dancer's cheek,
all the broken stomping, clapping,
duende of dark.

We stumbled out into the lighted lobby.
You grabbed my friend and me,
said we must all go now,
tonight, for *roja*,
wine for the dance and the darkness.

But we sad women demurred
to the rain in our hearts,
afraid of the blood call,
scurried like mice into hoods, coats,
another night we promised.

But it would not come again.
I knew then that I had
been called, chosen
and all these years have remembered
only what it was like not to go.

# THE TRANSPLANT

*for Ron Gower*

When you turn to me
my heart opens to receive the gift
like the heart of the young North Dakota man
that was cut out lovingly,
surgically precise,
and slipped into the empty
birdcage of our friend's chest
and set to beating again.

Whose face did this heart love?
In our friend's hospital sleep
does he dream of her now,
see her coming down the fence row,
her warm thighs and breasts making the heart beat faster,
making it swell and fly?

When you turn to me
all the pigeons of the world wheel and soar.
I open like the great cave,
like love, death. When you turn,
your hands on my heart
holding me, a shell to your chest,
she appears.
The world tumbles over and over.
I lift one languid arm,
the surgeon's knife
sliding into love.

# WEATHER IN THE NEW YEAR

*for John Mitchell*

Two black crows send greetings from the red-berried mountain ash.
After I die what I'll miss most: the touch of air on my skin.

When he wrote the Ninth Symphony
Beethoven was way past thought, beyond thinking.

Black beaks dive at deerskin humped on the road's shoulder.
Behind the trees something big and white, just ready to step out.

At the end we go into a deep non-being.
Surely the white birch still shines as lovingly.

At 63, almost 64, all I have are questions.
I never dreamed it would be this way.

## FIRE SONG

The universe has no edge
and no center.
Your DNA unraveled would reach
from here to the moon.
We are vulnerable to such beauty.
In the chaos of too much,
the arranging and rearranging of tables, chairs,
the all-night cremation fires smolder
separating atoms formed in the stars
that sparked into space and time.

What do grackles find in dead grass?
They gather, then fly away together
to a roof painted the color of flame.
Rustle and breath of fire.
Our Lady of Grackles.
Pilgrimage of seed and wing.
Oh, unnecessary skin!
The red-gold tulips are somnolent
in a cold March dusk.

Earlier, I had dug and dug,
found those bright green eyes already here.
What goes into the crucible is released,
a bolt of lightning on skin,
heat between my thighs,
hot on my forehead, my arms.
On the bed our sweat mingled when I was on fire.
I'd spend the whole day humming the fire song,
dragon tongue licking an ancient alphabet
of love and desire.

Soon moon, or no moon.
Bone-dark, black arms of cottonwood tree.
Only feather of candle
and the woman with wings standing
in the doorway.

# NOTES

I am indebted to Roseann Lloyd for the first two lines of "Persephone in Hades."

"Infiammati Fire Circus" is based on a performance given at Bedlam Theater in Minneapolis.

Lines in "The White Horse" are taken from Zen Master Dogen.

"Disambiguation" takes certain terminology from Wikipedia and Mozilla.

Lines in "Napalm, 2010" are from Bruce Weigl's poem "Song of Napalm" included in his book, *The Monkey Wars*.

"Dream of the Vietnamese Orphans": in the last days of the Vietnam War, Operation Babylift began the evacuation of orphans, many fathered by American GIs.

"Polar Bear": in June, 2008, the first polar bear to swim to Iceland in fifteen years was shot dead by police.

The sixth stanza in "Climbing Hverfjall Mountain" refers to the George Orwell essay, "A Hanging."

"Driving the Ring Road": dirty pants and scoria are types of volcanic rock.

"How It Begins" refers to the Intermezzo Opus 118, No. 2, by Johannes Brahms.

"The Memory Palace" takes its name from Simonides, the 6th century Greek poet credited with inventing this technique of "memory places" or method of loci.

"Cernunnos" is the horned god in Celtic mythology.

*Blood Wedding* refers to Carlos Saura's film of the play by Federico García Lorca.

photo: Sarah Aune

**Cary Waterman** is the author of four previous collections of poetry. Her poems are included in the anthologies *Poets Against the War, To Sing Along the Way: Minnesota Women Poets from Pre-territorial Days to the Present* and *Where One Song Ends, Another Begins: 150 Years of Minnesota Poetry.* She has received fellowships from the Minnesota State Arts Board, the Bush Foundation, the Loft and the McKnight Foundation. She lives in St. Paul and teaches creative writing at Augsburg College in Minneapolis.